Prof. Alfonso de Franciscis
Superintendent of Antiquities in Naples

POMPEII

Edizioni d'Arte
INTERDIPRESS - Via Galileo Ferraris, 132
Tel. 267311 - Napoli

Summary

Index of Views

HISTORICAL NOTES

The ancient Pompeii lies at the foot of Vesuvius, overlooking the River Sarno valley, not far from the sea. The site is particularly suitable for a human settlement as it is situated on the edge of a fertile agricultural area with good communication possibilities by land or sea. Owing to its position Pompeii was the natural sea landing place for the inland towns such as Nola, Nocera and Acerra and its port was perhaps at the mouth of the Sarno.

Infact Pompeii's prosperity through the centuries was due to its excellent topographic position. However the town did not have its own history and is seldom mentioned by the ancient writers, we must therefore reconstruct events in general terms especially making use of the data furnished by the archeological excavations. We know nothing certain of the first human settlements here but as in the Sarno valley evidence of life going back to the Iron Age has been found we can assume that in the IX-VIII century BC in the place where Pompeii was later to be established there was a village or groups of people — the ones who at that time populated the ancient Campania. As Pompeii established itself its contacts with the civilizations prospering in Campania became more frequent and enormously influenced the life of Pompeii. An important Etruscan centre, *Capua* was, infact not far away overlooking the plain of the River Volturno. Discussions continue as to how much the *Etruscans of Capua* influenced the life and history of Pompeii, but if as some writers say there was an etruscan period of the town, it is here in the oldest urbanistic arrangements, in the architecture and other manifestations of art and life that we find evidence of a continual and prolific contact between the Etruscan world and Pompeii. From the VI century BC the town was also influenced by the neighbouring Greek colonies, especially Cuma, and infact a Doric style temple was built in the Triangular Forum during this period.

However in the second half of the V century other Italic peoples, the Samnites, spread out from inland and settled in Campania. Pompeii was not spared from this invasion and, although we do not know the exact year, we believe the Samnite community was formed here about 425 BC. The town was later involved in the struggles between Rome and Sannio and in 310 the Pompeians together with the Nocerins repelled an attack from the Roman Navy. At the end of the war Pompeii allied itself to Rome and remained an ally during Hannibal's War.

During the Samnite period Pompeii enjoyed great economic prosperity founded mainly on agriculture and important urbanistic and artistic developments were made. The defensive system of the walls was fortified and new quarters with wide straight roads and large blocks of buildings were built. Existing public buildings had a facelift and new ones were constructed — the Triangular Forum was adorned with a porch and a colonnade and the doric temple, the theatre and the Odeon were rebuilt. In the centre of the town the civil Forum was surrounded by porches, the Temple of Jupiter and the Basilica erected whilst the Temple of Apollo was rebuilt. It was in this period that the construction began of large, rich, solidly built and nobly decorated atrium style private houses. However the revolt of the Italic allies against Rome involved Pompeii too. In 89 BC when occupied by Lucio Cluenzio's Italic armies, it was besieged by Silla and seized and in 80 BC it became a Roman colony with the name of *Colonia Cornelia Veneria Pompeiorum*. With this the history of Pompeii becomes part of Roman history and the town remains peaceful. Only one event in 59 AD is remembered when because of a brawl between the Pompeians and the Nocerins in the amphitheatre the Roman Senate decreed a suspension of all performances for 10 years. During this "Roman" period temples and public buildings were rebuilt and improved, among them the temple in honour of Augustus, another in honour of Vespian, the Eumachia building and the large Gymnasium while the amphitheatre dates back to the first years of the town as a Roman colony. The private building industry profited from contacts with Rome and the houses became more beautiful and comfortable and were decorated according to the current fashion. As industry and commerce grew consequently shops and works multiplied. But in 62 AD an earthquake destroyed many towns in Campania and Pompeii also suffered a lot of damage, evidence of which we can see in the buildings that the excavations have brought to light. Reconstruction work was difficult and although private persons' interest encouraged the prompt restoration of the houses and shops, seizing the opportunity to modernise rooms and decorations, the contrary can be said for the public buildings where work proceeded very slowly and many buildings were still unfinished when in 79 AD Vesuvius erupted.

This cataclysm, which buried Pompeii in a very short time, surprised the Pompeians as well as the inhabitants of other Vesuvian towns which fell victim. The fact is that they had not realised that

Vesuvius was a volcano — they considered it to be a green mountain with woods and vineyards. The catastrophe was terrible, and although many people suceeded in escaping, most of them could or would not and were killed by the poisonous gasses, by the falling buildings or by the rain of eruptive material. An exact description of the event is handed down by two letters that Plinio the Young wrote Tacito informing the famous historian about the death of his uncle Plinio the Old who was then chief of the Roman Navy at Misenum. Plinio the Old has seen the eruption from Misenum and had gone to the Vesuvian area both out of scientific curiosity and because he wanted to be of help — however when he arrived he to was killed. The archaelogical excavations allow us to live again those terrible moments. With a special method it is possible to reconstruct the Pompeian bodies and from the casts they appear in atrocious attitudes, in the act of escaping, trying to defend themselves from the poisonous gases with their clothes, carrying money or precious objects or seeking safety in flight through the ruins. Pompeii was buried by a blanket of ashes and lapilli more than 6 metres deep and the site was never re-inhabited — only a few surviviors or scoundrels returned to rummage and recover. The disaster touched the feelings and imagination of contemporaries and Marziale and Stazio remember it with very sorrowful verses while the Emperor Tito ordered special help for the area. In the middle ages Boethius mentions the disaster and later our humanists from Petrarca to Pontano and Sannazzaro remember it too.

The area was called *the Civita* as long as the memory of the buried town remained but it was only at the end of the 15th century that some traces of the buried town were brough to light and many years were to pass before regular digging was begun. It began, infact, in 1748 under the aegis of king Charles of Bourbon. Since then the excavation of Pompeii has not stopped and archaeologists study the evidence to gain an insight to the past giving humanity a spiritual patrimony of art and history which is unique.

A Map of
Pompeii

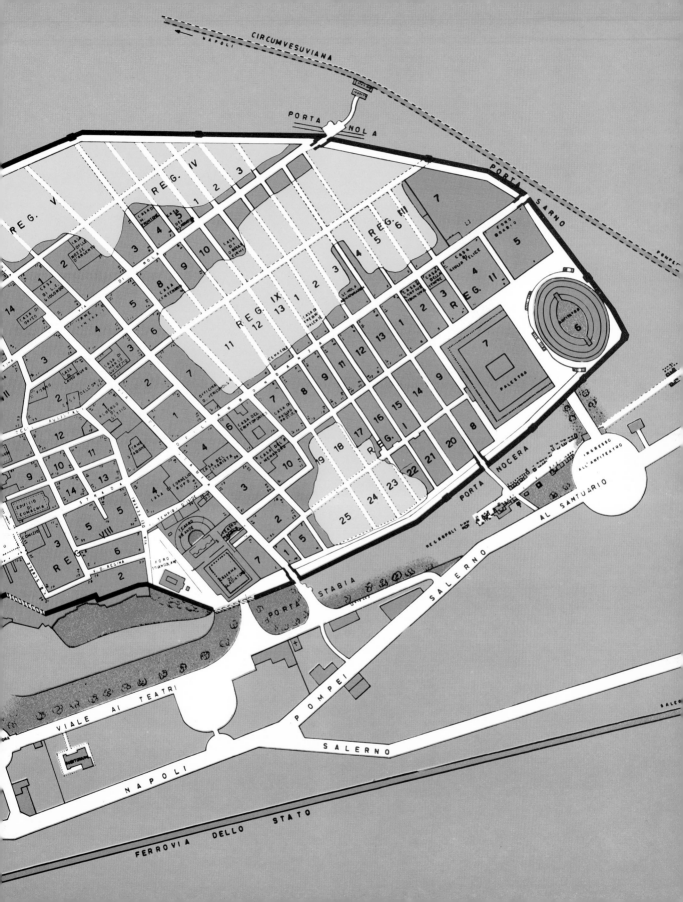

Walls and Gates

The fortifications of Pompeii are well preserved and we can see the entire perimeter and the structural characteristics of same. They were rebuilt many times from the VI to the I century BC but the from the appearance which were assumed in the Samnite period we can see a double curtain of square blocks reinforced by pillars and a support to which square cement towers were added in the last construction phase. Only the uppermost parts are missing which must have been crowned with a patrolway and battlements.

In correspondance with the main roads were the gates which have deep passage-ways often divided into two sectors lengthwise. Owing to the preservation Marina Gate, Stabiana Gate, Nolana Gate and Ercolanense Gate give us an exact idea of their original appearance while other gates although interesting were found to be almost entirely destroyed (Vesuvius Gate and Sarno Gate). Infact during the Roman period the walls and gates of Pompeii did not receive any particular care as they were no longer considered necessary during the climate of Roman peace. Many were actually demolished or incorporated into the houses and villas which were built on the town's edge. For the same reason, the damage caused by the earthquake to the gates was never repaired.

Roads

Pompeii gives us singular proof of the appearance of Roman roads and shows with what accuracy they were constructed. The roads are paved with a typical pavement of poligonal blocks of various shapes and sizes whilst a different method was used for paving large open areas. The Triangular Forum and the area between the amphitheatre and the Gymnasium are not paved but in the Civil Forum square the pavement which was renewed more than once is made up of large square slabs. It is also noteworthy that here and there stone blocks were placed transversally to obstruct passage at that point. Characteristic also is the frequent presence of large cut stones crossing the road from one side to another — these allowed pedestrians to cross the road without getting wet when rainwater flooded the road — between each stone is a narrow space allowing the wheels of the vehicles to pass. In fact Pompeii had a very limited sewerage system which was not sufficient to drain all the waste and rain-water. Evidence of the intense traffic in the town is given by the tracks, sometimes very deep that the frequent passage of vehicles has cut into the road paving. The roads were usually bordered by pavements which varied in breadth and in type of paving. In front of the richest houses the paving was particularly well cared for often with broken pottery mosaics. At many points on the edge of the pavement are holes where wooden poles were inserted to support curtains or tents put up in front of the houses or shops.

The Augustali Way and the Fountain

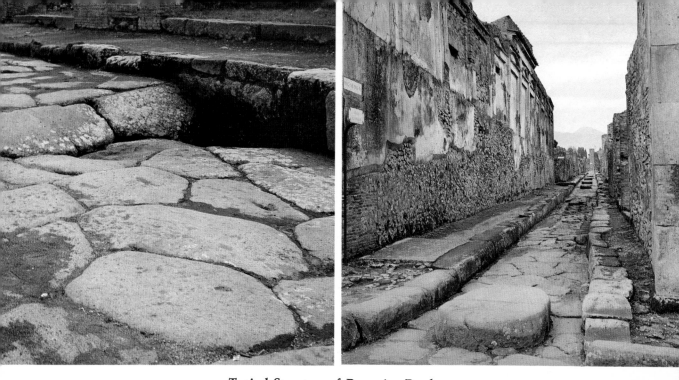

Typical Structure of Pompeian Roads

The Abundance Street

The Civil Forum

The centre of public life in Pompeii was the Forum, a large rectangular square stretching from north to south, with porches of difference ages and styles on three sides and all surrounded by public buildings. Here the Pompeians met for religious and political functions; to strike bargains or just to dally away their free time. A quick look at the buildings in the Forums shows us just how complex and animated daily life must have been. At the end of the square is the temple of Jupiter (father of gods and men) the most important worship place, here Juno and Minerva were also worshipped thus forming the traditional triad of Roman religion. The temple was built in the Samnite age during the second century BC and was later transformed by the Romans into the *Capitolium* of Pompeii. It is an Italic style temple, on a high podium the cell is preceded by a deep pronaos with a sacrifice altar in front. On each side of the temple are two arches erected in honour of members of the imperial family but we cannot identify them with any certainty.

On the western side of the square are the public barns, the municipal treasury seat, the place where measureswere controlled (*mensa ponderaria*) and finally the side of the sacred area where the temple of Apollo is situated. This is a place of worship going back at least of the VI century BC but nowadays we see it as it appeared in the Samnite age with restorations made during the Roman period. To the south of the Forum are the public administration buildings, the seat of the duoviri, the most important magistrates in the town, that of master builders and the Senate house where the town Council assembled. Not far away stands the *Comitium*, an area used for elections. On the eastern side of the square is a building built at the expense of the priestess Eumachia — this was the seat of one of the most prosperous guilds in Pompeii, the *fullones'* who were manufacturers of woollen cloth. The there is a small temple dedicated, it seems, to the emperor Vespasian and a small temple in honour of Public Lares. Next door is the *Macellum*, a large market with shops and also a shrine devoted to imperial worship.

In the neighbourhood of the square are other public buildings, the temple of *Fortuna Augusta* devoted to a religious cult characteristic of the Roman imperial world as well as the Forum thermae and the Basilica.

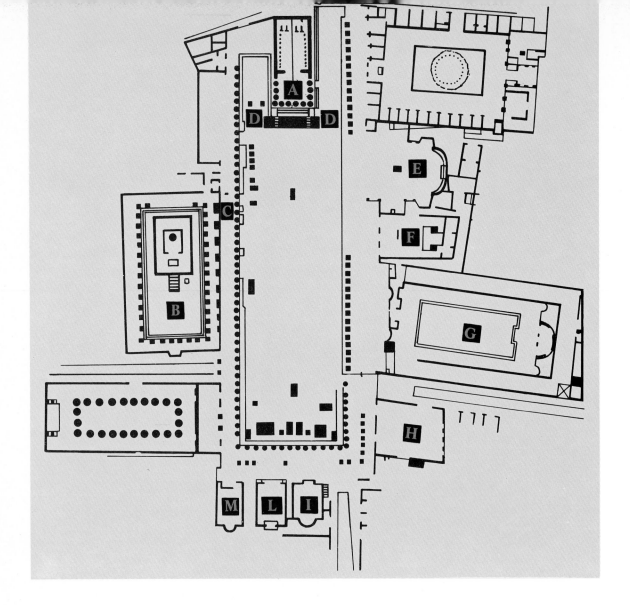

The plan of the Imperial Forum

A The Temple of Jupiter
B The Temple of Apollo
C Ponderaria Table
D Honorary Arches
E The Temple of Lares

F The Temple of Vespasian
G The Building of Eumachia
H Comitium
I Duumviri's Office
L Senate-House

M Aediles' Office

The Forum Civile

The Temple of Apollo - Detail

The Arch of Germanicus

The Civil Forum - Western Ambulacrum

The Civil Forum - Eastern Ambulacrum

The Temple of the Fortuna Augusta

The Civil Forum

Temple of Vespasian
ᵛ

The Forum Street and The Arch of Caligula

The Jupiter Temple
∨

The Basilica

The Basilica stands at the southwest end of the Forum, the main entrance is preceded by a vestibule, the *chalcidicum*, while there are another two entrance doors at the sides. Inside there is a brick colonnade at the end of which stands the tribunal a high podium with double superimposed columns crowned by a fronton. The building, the walls of which are decorated in the first Pompeian style, dates back to the last years of the second century BC but the earthquake in 62 BC destroyed it and it was never rebuilt. Many scholars think the Basilica was once covered with a double sloping roof but it is more probable that the internal colonnade formed a continuous porch which surrounded an open central area. Here judgements were made, bankers, merchants and businessmen met to discuss business and like the Forum square this was one of the busiest places in Pompeii.

The Basilica

The Triangular Forum

The large square which we usually call the triangular forum has gathered around it other monuments of Pompeii — for example the two theatres and the Samnite gymnasium and in the middle are the remains of a doric temple. This temple goes back to the VI century BC and shows the contact Pompeii had at this time with the Greek towns in Southern Italy and in particular Cuma. The temple was restored in the IV-III century BC but later it was probably neglected and in the Roman age it had become a simple chapel. We do not know the gods to which it was dedicated but during the last period Hercules and Minerva were worshipped here. On the whole the Triangular Forum shows a noble architecture of the Samnite age with a high colonnaded vestibule and a doric arcade surrounding the square.

Triangular Forum   **Aerial view of the excavations** ➤

The Isis' Temple

The worship of Isis originally introduced from Egypt was common in Pompeii. This divinity's sanctuary stands near the Triengular Forum with a high wall and simple entrance determining the sacred area where the religious cerimonies took place. The little temple stands on a high podium and the sacred object of the Isis cult were kept in the cell, the altar is near the flight of stairs. In the south-east corner of the sacred area is a small room leading to an underground cavity where the water of the Nile was kept and on the other side in another covered area the ashes and remains of the sacrifices were gathered. Behind the temple is a large room which was used as a meeting place for the worshippers, the number of which was considerable in Pompeii. We do not know when this religious cult was introduced in Pompeii but the sanctuary as we see it was rebuilt by Numerio Popidio Celsino after the earthquake in 62 BC.

The Temple of Isis

Thermae

Three important thermal establishments stand at the cross-roads of the most important thoroughfares in Pompeii, they are the "Stabiane" thermae, the "Forum" thermae and the "Central" thermae. The oldest is the Stabiane thermae which was built in the Samnite age but later enlarged and radically renewed to meet the new hygenic and social requirements of the Romans. The old nucleus consisted of a large comunal room and a row of smaller rooms each with a basin and a brazier. The later complex includes a large yard surrounded by arcades which was used as a Gymnasium and the thermal places were divided, as was the rule at that time, into male and female areas. Each thermal area was traditionally divided into: dressing rooms (*apodyterium*), *frigidarium*, *tepidarium* and *calidarium*. Heat circulated through the empty spaces under the floor which was supported on brick columns (suspensurae) and in the hollow spaces between the walls. The heat was produced in the

The Central Courtyard

Forum Thermae

furnace which was situated between the male and female sections, the water being boiled in cylindrical boilers. On the other side of the courtyard is an open air pool and rooms used as dressing rooms and restrooms for the athletes. The Stabiane thermae were severely damaged by the earthquake in 62 BC and most of the painted decorations were lost, however most of the plaster decorations dating back to the last years of Pompeii remain. The Forum thermae is a reproduction of a smaller scale of the Stabiane thermae but the decoration is more refined. After the earthquake a new thermal establishment — the Central thermae was begun but never finished. All in bricks the building shows that it would have been a new architectural conception with wide areas and large windows for light and air and a single thermal area without divisions for male and female bathing.

Theatres, Amphitheatre

Pompeii already had a building for theatrical performances in about the V century BC — it was a simple structure which made use of the natural land slope as the Greeks did and had a wooden stage. Over the centuries it was renewed many times, in the Samnite age tufa seats for the spectators were built and in the Roman age the flight of steps was enlarged and the stage rebuilt in stone with an articulated scenic front like the theatres in the larger towns in Italy and Asia Minor. Many of these adjustments were made thanks to the generosity of famous Pompeian citizens such as M. Antonio Primo, M. Olconio Rufo and M. Olconio Celere.

We now see the theatre as it was after the last restoration in the Augustan age. The *cavea* with seats for the spectators is partially supported by a covered passage and to the sides are the *tribunalia* for the more important spectators. The orchestra pit which was no longer used for player's action was occupied by spectators as well. The stage is composed of a low stage where the actors recited and stately background with nooks, aediculas and three doors opening like the front of a palace, columns, tympanum and statues all helped to make the scene more attractive.

The theatre could hold about 5000 spectators. Behind the stage was a square porched area where spectators stopped or sought shelter when the weather was bad.

The Odeon stands near the theatre, it is a similar structure but much smaller and was used for artistic performances which attracted a smaller public, such as musical auditions, recitation of lines and miming and infact could hold less than 1000 people. It was rebuilt about 80 BC thanks to the generosity of C. Quinzio Valgo and M. Porcio and after this was never again renewed. The flight of steps has been very well preserved and remains a noble example of the late Hellenistic taste flourishing in Pompeii and in other areas during the last two centuries BC. The tufa telamones decorating the end of the *cavea* are interesting examples of the sculpture of this period.

At the same time and thanks once again to the generosity of C. Quinzio Valgo and M. Porcio the amphitheatre was built which could hold 20,000 spectators and this is the oldest Roman amphitheatre which we know. The building is partially enclosed by land but it has no cellars and the entrance to the flight of steps

The small Theatre or Odeon

have outer steps. Here we do not find the complicated structure
which characterizes the amphitheatres of the first imperial Roman
period.
Near the amphitheatre there is a large Gymnasium surrounded by
porches and a swimming pool in the centre — here gladiators train-
ed as the many graffiti testify.

The Large Theatre -
The Odeon - The Gymnasium

Large Theatre

▲ The Amphitheatre

◄ Large Gymnasium

32

The Houses and Villas

The excavation of a town like Pompeii offers us a large and varied assortment of private houses. The commonest type is the "atrium" house, characteristic of the Italic-Roman milieu. The central nucleus is formed by a large atrium with a roof open in the centre (*compluvium*) and a basin to gather the rain-water (*impluvium*). Around the atrium the rooms (*cubicula*) are situated and at the end, facing the entrance (*fauces*) there is the *tablinium* and behind this a green area — an orchard or garden (*hortus*) opens. As the house has almost no windows on the outside it appears completely closed from the outside. This type of house which may be small and modest or large and rich received in the second century BC the influence of the Greek Hellenistic type house and replaced the *hortus* with a large peristyle which was a garden enclosed by porches and rooms. Thus it can be seen that the principal nucleus with its various parts, the triclinium, hall and bedrooms is transferred to this part of the house. Those rooms along the road which were not used for dwelling opened onto the road as shops or workshops. Many houses, especially the richer ones also had an upper storey used for other dwellings and rooms for the servants. The rooms had floors with decorations which ranged from simple broken earthware pieces to mosaic work and of course the walls were decorated with murals which have become famous during the excavation of Pompeii. On the outskirts of the town and outside the walls we can see another type of house — the villa. Here the arrangement of the rooms varies and usually depends on the conditions of the soil and the desire to have large gardens and a panoramic view. The atrium is often smaller but the rear part received more attention and infact opens out to become part of the countryside. In these villas, more so than in the houses we find bathing facilities and areas reserved for agricultural activities, stables, cellars etc. The *suburban* villas and farms scattered on the outskirt of the town are larger and more varied.

The Vettis' House

This house belonged to a family of rich merchants and reflects the tenor of life of the wealthy class of Pompeii in the first century AD. In the atrium are two safes and all around are rooms decorated with pictures of mythological subjects in the IV Pompeian style. The house has no tablinum but the peristyle receives more attention. Here the garden has been reconstructed with elements furnished by the excavations and plants and fountains so it appears as it must have looked originally. The rooms which open out here are decorated with fine murals and the tricliniar room is one of the most refined examples of Pompeian decoration — the walls have a red background split up by banded pillars and all around runs a frieze depicting Amoretti in everyday activities such as the selling of oil, biga racing, goldsmiths at work, gathering grapes, the wine market etc. The servants quarter with an upper storey is concentrated around a secondary atrium and there is also a flat with a porch reserved for the women.

The Vettis' House - Peristylium (detail)

**Ornamentation
with Amoretti**

**The Vintners
Amoretti**

**The Goldsmiths
Amoretti**

35

The Pansa's House

When it was first built in the Samnite age this house occupied the whole block and belonged to one family, probably the *Arriana Polliana* family. It was later divided into more than one house and is therefore interesting evidence of the development of the private building industry which we can note in Pompeii by the middle of the first century AD. At that time prevailing agricultural economy with important landowners was almost replaced by a commercial and industrial economy which changed the social structure of the town.

Of the primitive nucleus of this house only the large atrium and peristyle in the centre of which is a large basin remain. Behind this block is the *hortus* and infact the excavations have revealed traces of ancient cultivation. In this house have also been found proof that a christian community gathered there in the first years of the diffusion of this new religion in Italy.

The Pansa's House - Peristylium

The Faunus' House

This house, as we see it now, is a remarkable example of private architecture of the Samnite period and dates back to the second century BC but the original foundations go back as far as the fifth century BC. The architecture is noble and harmonious and recalls Hellenistic taste while the wall decoration is moderate and refined in the first Pompeian style with bright plaster squares imitating marble plates. The rooms have mosaic floors which are amongst the best we know, the most famous being the mosaic depicting a battle between Alexander the Great and Darius the Persian King. We can consider these mosaics although not Hellenistic orinals very good reproductions. The house takes its name from the little statue of the Faunus in the impluvium which is a Greek original of the third-second century BC and probably belonged to the *Cassia Family.*

The Faunus' House - Atrium

The House of the golden Amoretti

This house belonged to the Poppei family which was one of the most important in Pompeii and related to the Emperor Nero. The plant and decoration of the house testify to a particularly good artistic taste — the atrium is of the Tuscan type but the most interesting part is the peristyle. As usual rooms for everyday activities are situated all around but one side is slightly elevated and appears to be the stage of a theatre with three entrances. We therefore think that this family cultivated dramatic art and here plays for a small selected audience were performed. There is also a chapel in honour of Isis, singular but not unique evidence of private worship to an Egyptian divinity in Pompeii.

The House of the Golden Amoretti · Peristylium

The Tragic Poet's House

This is a small but tasteful house is characteristic of a house of the Pompeian middle class which passed through a fortunate period during the last years of Pompeii. It is also one of the most famous houses of Pompeii and very dear to Roman age literature. Here can be found two famous mosaics, the first decorating the entrance represents a dog tied with a chain and has an inscription *"Cave canem"* and the second in the tablinum shows a group of players preparing for a performance. There are also fine mythological paintings showing the deserted Arianna, Arianna and Teseo, Venus, Narcissus and finally a picture of Iphigenia's sacrifice which has excited scholars who see it as a derivation of a famous painting of Timante who was a famous Greek painter of the fifth and fourth century BC. This house also had an upper storey of which many traces have been found during the excavation.

The Lucrezio Frontone's House

The main point of interest in M.L. Frontone's house is its wall decoration which is extremely well preserved and constitutes an excellent example of Pompeian painting going back to the first imperial age. Other mythological paintings decorating the rooms are justly famous, for example Bacchus' triumphal retinue, Narcissus at the spring, Teseo and Arianna and Oresetes in Delphi. The house belonged to well-to-do people as we note from the decorations and the variety of rooms surrounding the atrium and in the rear around the garden is a summer triclinium. On the wall at the end of the garden is a large painting showing animals and trees in an African landscape.

◄ House of Lucretius Fronto

The Ceis' House

This house (the owner was L. Ceio Secondo) from its simple design evident especially in the four columned atrium and the decorations in the old Pompeian style goes back to the pre-roman age but underwent radical changes in later times. Infact an upper storey was added which was reached by a stairway leading from the atrium and divided by a gallery. This newer construction was carried out in a rustic style with a simple frame and is an interesting example of building transformation in private houses in Pompeii. In the atrium there was a wooden wardrobe, tracing of which has been obtained with the special method used in the excavations in Pompeii. At the end of the house is a small garden the walls of which are decorated with a large painting of a landscape with animals and trees.

The Menander's House

This is one of the finest Pompeian houses with noble architectural proportions and a detailed plan. Another branch of the Poppei family which we have already met in the house of the Golden Amoretti, lived here. The facade facing on to the road is adorned with two tufa pillars with Corinthian capitals. The atrium is in the Tuscan style and the walls are decorated in the last Pompeian style. In one corner is a little chapel for the worship of the domestic gods. Many rooms open out onto the atrium and one of them is decorated with little pictures of episodes from the "Illyad" — Laocoön, the Trojan horse and Cassandra. Gathered around the peristyle which is at the rear are still more rooms. From one side we can see a large triclinium where the excavations have been carried out in layers showing the first construction phase of the house with wall decorations of the first style. In a small room nearby skeletons of the victims of the eruption have been found. Next come the servants quarters where the slaves lived and then the rustic lodgings and a small courtyard with a stable. At the end of the peristyle we can see paintings of theatrical subjects including a portrait of the poet Menander and from this the house gets its name. From the other side of the peristyle it is possible to reach the bathroom which reproduces on a smaller scale and with refined pictorial decorations a typical thermal complex. The silver plate found in this house testifies to the wealth of the inhabitants.

Peristylium ∧

Atrium ➤

43

The House of the Large Fountain

The house of the large fountain and that of the small fountain derives its name from a special ornament which is found in the garden. From a stone nook covered with vitreous polychrome mosaic work springs a fountain the water of which gathers in a small basin covered with marble plates. Small bronze statues and marble masks all help to make the effect more lively. It is not easy to recover mosaic wall decorations such as these during archaelogical excavations — much more common are the mosaic floors — this is because these wall decorations are more susceptible to damage and ruin. Thus we sometimes get the wrong impression that the ancients used mosaics only for floor decorations but here Pompeii gives us a valuable idea of wall mosaics.

The Large Fountain - Detail

The House of the Large Fountain - Nympheum in Mosaic ➤

The House of Venus in the Shell

Here the construction is concentrated around the garden along which there is a two-sided porch. On the end wall is an airy, vivid painting with subjects relating to the garden — hedges with flowery bushes, marble basins with doves and even a Mars. The large composition in the centre of the painting is Venus sailing the sea in a shell and escorted by two Amoretti. Artistically speaking this is a modest work but must be appreciated for its decorative taste which harmonises pleasantly with the garden and its flora.

The House of the Orchard

The vivid decoration which gives the name to this house (also called "the house of the floral cubicles") adorns the walls of two cubicles, one near the atrium and the other near the tablinum. The paintings show fig-trees, cherry-trees, strawberry trees and lemon-trees which must have been rare in ancient Campania — birds and other animals give life to the picture which undoubtedly was inspired by the fertile Pompeian countryside of that period. In the lower part of the painting trees, basins, enclosures give the idea of a garden and the fact that these subjects have been used for a painting inside the house and not in the garden or porch suggest that the house was inhabited by a rich fruitgrower who chose subjects close to his daily life. From Egyptian subjects found in the same cubicles it is also thought that worship of Dionysus-Osiris was practised here.

The Loreio Tiburtino's House

This is a house of simple, harmonious proportions and a large part is given over to the green of the garden which stretches out at the back of the house and to the long loggia covered by a pergola. A stream with a small waterfall, fountains and statues of muses, animals and hermas adorned the whole setting. At the end of the loggia, in the open air, a triclinium is decorated with mythical subjects Pyramus and Thisbe and Narcissus and even if these paintings have no artistic value they are interesting as they were signed by the artist and man called *Lucius*. The paintings in the hall were painted with more care — on two uninterrupted freizes are depicted the Trojan cycle and the labours of Hercules. In another small room is an elegant painting of many figures one of which is the figure of a priest of Isis and is thought to be the portrait of one of the inhabitants of the house.

The Garden

The Giulia Felice's House

This house was built at the east end of the town and its several parts surround a large garden which is bordered on one side by a marble pillared porch and on the other by a pergola whilst in the centre is a large pool. Behind the porch are many rooms one of which is the triclinium and then the thermal quarter which we learn from the inscription was let for public use. Here we can recognise the characteristic elements — *frigidarium*, *tepidarium*, *calidarium* and a *laconicum* for *sudationes*. Nearby is a block used for shops which had an upper storey and finally behind the villa is a large area with a kitchen garden and an orchard.

Porch and Garden

The Diomede's Villa

This villa opens out onto the Graves Way with a small entrance which leads into the peristyle around which are situated the various parts of the villa. To the east is the thermal quarter with a small porch and a pool for cold baths while to the north and south are a succession of rooms including the triclinium and an apse hall with three large windows. Opposite the entrance is the tablinium which leads on to the other part of the villa formed by a garden in a square area surrounded by porches supporting a balcony while in the centre of the garden is a pool and a summer triclinium. This is a classic example of an urban villa plan in the imperial roman age.

The Peristylium

The suburban Villa of Marina Gate

A suburban villa standing near the Marina Gate is sometimes mistakenly called the Imperial Villa. It was built making use of the defensive wall when this no longer had a defensive task and is constructed in terraces so as to appreciate the surrounding panorama. The villa was partially destroyed in 62 BC but still shows evidence today of its complex architectural design. A long porch with paintings of the third style surround the garden and led to the bedrooms, a triclinium hall and other rooms. The hall, preceded by a vestibule and bordered by passages is one of the largest covered rooms we know in Pompeian buildings and contains fine paintings showing scenes of Teseo and Icarus. The villa which has not been completely excavated must have been large and rich with other rooms, porches and a garden of which we only know a part.

So called Imperial Villa · Detail of the Porch

The Villa of Mysteries

This is perhaps the most famous and most highly admired house in Pompeii because it is the finest and most complete example of a large suburban villa and also because of its various rooms decorated with artistically superior paintings especially in the triclinium hall which contains the famous freize which gives the villa its name. The excavation of this villa which began in 1909-10 is not yet complete but it is thought that the small part still buried can add little to what we already know. The first plan of the villa goes back to the second century BC but was later enlarged and rebuilt as a luxury house and its golden moment came during the Augustan Age when it became part of the imperial state property. However after the earthquake it was reduced to a rustic villa and its last owners belonged to the Istacidi family. It is a large four-sided bulding built on a slope so that it rests partially on the

Peristylium   **The Villa of Mysteries - The Sacrifice and Silenus playing ➤**

ground and partially on a covered porch. The entrance, not completely excavated leads onto a road of which we know only a small part and which was perhaps linked to the Graves Way. To the sides of the entrance are the servants quarters with equipment for making pasta, also an oven, the kitchens, wine pantry and a wine press. From the entrance passing through a small atrium we reach the peristyle where the true nucleus of this house begins with rooms and halls for different uses and a group of thermal rooms. Here is the large atrium, the tablinium and an apse verandah with a view of the sea. To the sides are still more rooms, cubicles, the triclinium with the famous large freize and porches dividing different groups of rooms. Passing through the verandah to visit the villa we note that this part of the buildings has hanging gardens and is supported by the aforementioned covered porch. The painted wall decorations have unequalled interest and reflect the different periods of the building's life and the various uses it was put to. The decorations of the III and IV styles are less interesting but the tablinum is noteworthy with its black walls and Egyptian type symbols — however the most valuable are the paintings of the second style which were spared the changes the villa underwent during the last period. A cubicle with figures linked to the myth and worship of Dionysus is decorated in the same style and this cubicle is used as an anteroom for the triclinium hall. The large freize in this hall is of the second style and is the most complete example of a special type which we seldom see in the paintings of this period — here infact is a continuous representation which occupies all the walls in the rooms with natural size figures. This freize was perhaps executed towards the middle of the first century BC by a local artist who drew inspiration from the works of Greek painters or was influenced by that style of painting and its classical rules. Scholars cannot agree to the paintings' meaning as it does not deal with an easily identifiable subject — it is composed of different scenes one after the other which deal with different stages of a rite about which we have no information. It is believed that the painting is related to the mistery worship which existed together in the Greek-Roman world with the state religion but which was known only by a few selected men. Many people believe that the freize deals with the various phases of the initiation of a bride to dionysiac mysteries — mysteries which were found in Campania in the Roman age. Thus we see in the various scenes both human and divine figures. The

The Scourged and the naked Bacchanite ➤

Reading of the Ritual and young Girl offering

reason why the frezie was painted here can be explained by the fact that the ladyowner was an iniator and minister of this cult. The freize begins on the north wall near a small door — in the first scene a boy is reading the sacred ritual under the guidance of a noble lady while a woman in a mantle listens. The next scene depicts the sacrifice and offering with a pastoral group including Silenus playing the lyre.

The wall at the end of the hall is dominated by two divinities to whom the rites are relative, Dionysus and Arianna, then to one side Silenian satyrs are intent on some mysterious deed whilst on the other side a woman reveals the symbol of fertility whilst a winged figure is in the act of striking with a *flagellum*. On another wall a whipped woman seeks refuge in her friends lap whilst nearby a naked Bacchanite dances seized by orgiastic excitement. Lastly the bride dresses and the rite ends showing her sitting and mantled now the initiated and mystic bride of the god.

Preparation for initiation to the Mysteries

Mills, Wines and Shops

The shops and workshops in Pompeii offer us a valuable insight into the daily life of the Pompeians and help to clarify what the contemporary writers wrote. Not only daily life with its vivid human aspects but also social and economic life with all its fascinating problems and multiform aspects. The shops and workshops set in rows along the roads of the town occupy the ground floor rooms which have often only been transformed into shops during the last years of Pompeii when the merchants fluorished and the rich families began to decline. Often we can see that a mezzanine wooden floor had been constructed to provide an abode for the seller (we still see this practice in our southern towns) and signs often remain of a small wooden porch which overlooked the road. On the outer wall of the shops we can note painted signs which drew

Mill and Oven

Shops

passer-by's attention to what was sold in that particular shop or signs depicting divinities who it was hoped would help and protect the shop. Inside the shops and workshops we can gather from the furniture and equipment as well as painted or graphite inscriptions what was sold there. At the entrance to the shops a long stone bench covered with marble or painted plaster was used to exhibit the goods — bulging amphoras on the counter held corn, oil and wine and sometimes residues of the contents have been found during the excavations. A product found in the well-sealed amphoras is the *garum* a kind of fish sauce and we can read the name of the sauce and the manufacturer of the sauce on the amphoras. From all this evidence we can find out the agricultural production of the area, the goods imported and the diet of the Pompeians. We must not forget the many *tabernae*, really public-houses and the *thermopolia* which rather looked like our bars — these were places where people met for a drink and a chat. One of these establishments was managed not by a landlord but by girls who seemed to have been activists during the last Pompeian elections. The bakeries have also proved to be very interesting — we can see the mill stones with which they produced the flour and nearby the table where the dough was kneaded and at the end of the room the oven. Pieces of carbonized bread have been found during the excavations and also an inscription testifying to the goodness of Pompeian bread. Obviously all the most important activities are recognizable in the shops — bread was sold either at the bakery where it was produced or in special bakershops, there were fruiteres one of whom was a certain *Felix*, vegetable sellers, shoemakers, washerwoman and dyers, carpenters and blacksmiths and pastry cooks who judging from the cake forms found must have been very skillful. To complete the picture we have the brothel giving us an interesting insight into the morals and the *hospitium* a modest inn organization for people who came from a distance place.

▲ Tracings of corpses foud in a garden

Sepulchral Monuments

The principal roads connecting Pompeii with neighbouring towns were bordered, as was the classic custom, not only by villas and country houses but also by sepulchral areas, the necropolis. Side by side with poor graves are several rich sepulchral monuments which belonged to personages who held an important place in the history or public life of the town as well as to the most influential Pompeian families. Styles vary, some reflect Greek-Hellenistic funeral architecture while others follow the Roman Italic tradition and yet others reflect particular tastes and requirements. Often the points of greater distinction from the artistic point of view are found in the sepulchral enclosure which is surrounded by a low wall and included a small open area for burials in the earth and a columbarium room where the urns for ashes were kept. Two extraurban roads outside Pompeii possess the majority of these monuments, they are Sepulchre or Tomb Way leading from the Herculaneum Gate and the Nucerina Way but others have also been found outside Stabia Gate, Vesuvious Gate and places more distant from the town. Along the Sepulchre Way we can see: the *Istacidis* Mausoleum — a circular temple set on a high podium and adorned with statues only one of which survives today, then there is the Tomb of Garlands one of the most ancient with its fine relief decoration, *M. Umbricio Scauro's Sepulchre* showing scenes from gladiator games in his honour, *C. Munazio Fausto* and his wife *Nevoleia Tyche's* sepulchre including a marble altar on which are sculpted a funeral ceremony and a ship lowering the sails — an important example of sculpture of the last years of Pompeii. Here also is the *Family Ceia's* sepulchre adorned with statues. No less interesting are the sepulchres found along the Nucerina Way; the *Cuspis* sepulchre with a columbarium room on top of which stands a circular monument, this same circular monument is found inside the funeral enclosure of the *Veia Barchilla's Sepulchre*. There is the funeral area belonging to the *Flavia family* who were freedmen with aediculas showing their dead's portraits and a square temple sepulchre which has statues of the dead in sitting positions, also the large exedra sepulchre of the priestess *Eumachia*, *M. Ottavio* and his relatives' monument formed by a four colonnaded temple with the dead's statues, the *Stronnis' Sepulchre* like a podium with crouched lions executed in the Hellenistic style and *Vesonis'* aedicula monument again with statues of their dead. All these funeral monuments usually have inscriptions telling us the names and rank of the per-

The street of the Tombs

The tomb of the Istachidi

63

sonages buried there and in this way we can see the activity they carried out in Pompeii, follow episodes in their life, identify their house, the public works they performed and finally the place where they are buried.

ALFONSO DE FRANCISCIS
Superintendent of Antiquities in Naples